57144

**Butterfield School
Learning Center
1441 W. Lake Street
Libertyville, IL 60048**

EXPLORING COUNTRIES

Denmark

by Derek Zobel

BELLWETHER MEDIA · MINNEAPOLIS, MN

Note to Librarians, Teachers, and Parents:

Blastoff! Readers are carefully developed by literacy experts and combine standards-based content with developmentally appropriate text.

Level 1 provides the most support through repetition of high-frequency words, light text, predictable sentence patterns, and strong visual support.

Level 2 offers early readers a bit more challenge through varied simple sentences, increased text load, and less repetition of high-frequency words.

Level 3 advances early-fluent readers toward fluency through increased text and concept load, less reliance on visuals, longer sentences, and more literary language.

Level 4 builds reading stamina by providing more text per page, increased use of punctuation, greater variation in sentence patterns, and increasingly challenging vocabulary.

Level 5 encourages children to move from "learning to read" to "reading to learn" by providing even more text, varied writing styles, and less familiar topics.

Whichever book is right for your reader, Blastoff! Readers are the perfect books to build confidence and encourage a love of reading that will last a lifetime!

This edition first published in 2011 by Bellwether Media, Inc.

No part of this publication may be reproduced in whole or in part without written permission of the publisher.
For information regarding permission, write to Bellwether Media, Inc., Attention: Permissions Department,
6325 Sandburg Road, Suite 200, Minneapolis, MN 55427.

Library of Congress Cataloging-in-Publication Data

Contents

Where Is Denmark?

North
Sea

Did you know?
Greenland is over 50 times larger than Denmark!

Sweden

Denmark

Copenhagen ★

Zealand

Funen

Germany

4

Denmark is a small country in northern Europe that covers 16,639 square miles (43,094 square kilometers). It takes up part of the Jutland **peninsula** and includes over 440 surrounding islands. Two of the largest islands are Zealand and Funen. Denmark's capital, Copenhagen, lies on Zealand.

Denmark shares its southern border with Germany. It touches the North Sea to the west and the Baltic Sea to the east. The Scandinavian Peninsula, which includes Norway and Sweden, lies across the sea to the north. Denmark claims Greenland and the Faroe Islands as overseas **territories**. Greenland lies northeast of Canada, and the Faroe Islands are north of Scotland.

Baltic Sea

The land in Denmark is mostly flat, but some rolling hills fill the center of the Jutland. Sandy beaches and long, narrow **fjords** are scattered along Denmark's coastline. The largest fjord in the country is the Lim Fjord. It lies in the northern part of the Jutland.

Denmark's longest river, the Guden, flows through the peninsula in the north. This river passes through many of the country's lakes as it makes its way to Randers Fjord and then the ocean. The Vida River, located in southern Denmark, stretches along the border between Denmark and Germany.

fun fact

Kronborg is a fortress that lies on the Danish side of Oresund. It controlled access to the Baltic Sea for hundreds of years.

Between Sweden and the Jutland lie the Danish **straits**. People in Denmark and other northern European countries have used these straits as **shipping lanes** for many years.

The Danish straits connect the Baltic Sea to the North Sea. The western strait is called the Little Belt. It lies between the Jutland and the island of Funen. The middle strait is the widest. It is called the Great Belt and stretches between Funen and Zealand. Oresund, the eastern strait, separates Zealand from the coast of Sweden.

North Sea

Sweden

Oresund

Denmark

Great Belt

Little Belt

Zealand

Funen

Baltic Sea

fallow deer

Denmark has a wide variety of wildlife. In the forests and flat plains, wolves and brown bears hunt roe, red, and fallow deer. The European polecat and pine marten, two weasel-like animals, also make their homes in these areas.

brown bear

garfish

European polecat

Off the coasts of Denmark, dolphins, whales, and many kinds of fish swim. Salmon and sea trout fill the rivers throughout the country. In the Danish straits, flatfish and garfish swim in large numbers.

Danish people are called Danes. Over 5.5 million people live in Denmark. Most of these people claim the **Germanic peoples** of Europe as their **ancestors**. Some people in Denmark are **immigrants**. They come from countries in southwest Asia, especially Turkey.

Speak Danish!

English	Danish	How to say it
hello	hej	high
good-bye	farvel	far-vill
yes	ja	yah
no	nej	nigh
please	venligst	VEN-ligst
thank you	tak	tock
friend	ven	vin

fun fact

The Inuit often wear their traditional clothing to keep warm in the cold weather.

The official language of Denmark is Danish. Many Danes near the border with Germany speak German, and a lot of Danes also speak English. The Inuit in Greenland have their own language and customs. On the Faroe Islands, the **Nordic peoples** speak Faroese.

fun fact

Copenhagen is known as "The City of Bikes" because of the large number of public bicycles there.

Most Danish people live in and around cities. They live in modern houses or apartments and shop at local markets and malls. Many cities have buses and trains that people use to get around town. Some cities provide free public bicycles that people can ride from place to place.

In the countryside, people live in small towns or on farms. They use cars and trucks to get around. If they have to go to a larger city, they often take a train.

Where People Live in Denmark

countryside 13%

cities 87%

The Danish government requires children to go to school from kindergarten through ninth grade. Tenth grade is optional, but many Danish students choose to attend. Students in these grades study math, Danish, science, art, and other subjects.

After finishing ninth or tenth grade, students can take an exam and continue with school. Some students go to schools that prepare them for specific jobs. Others study to go to a university.

Did you know?
The Copenhagen University Library was founded in 1582. It is the oldest library in Denmark.

Where People Work in Denmark

manufacturing 20%

farming 3%

services 77%

Did you know?

Many Danes find work as fishermen and sell their catches in markets and to restaurants.

18

! **fun fact**
Denmark was one of the first countries to use wind power. Almost half of the wind turbines used around the world are made in Denmark.

Denmark has very few **natural resources**, so most Danish people have **service jobs**. They work in banks, hospitals, and schools. They also work in hotels, restaurants, and museums that serve **tourists**.

In the countryside, people work on farms or in mines. Farmers grow barley, wheat, and other crops. They make milk, cheese, and butter. Miners dig up metals, limestone, and other **minerals** to send to factories in the cities. There, they are made into products that are shipped all over the world.

19

fun fact

LEGOs were invented in Denmark in the 1950s. The word *LEGO* comes from the Danish phrase *leg godt*, which means "play well."

Danish people play many sports. Soccer is a favorite of all ages. Handball, rugby, and tennis are also popular throughout the country. Most schools and cities have sports clubs that people can join.

Denmark's landscapes allow for many outdoor activities. Danish people fish and kayak in rivers, streams, and lakes. Cyclists race across the country's flat plains and rolling hills. Off the coasts, many Danish people enjoy sailing in the North and Baltic seas.

fun fact

In Danish bakeries, people make pastries that are topped or filled with chocolate, fruits, or custard. These pastries, called "Danishes," are popular around the world.

Dairy products, fruits, fish, and bread make up the majority of the Danish **diet**. Bread and cheese are eaten throughout the day. In the morning, Danes enjoy yogurt, coffee or tea, and bread with jam or cheese. For lunch, Danes often eat *smørrebrød*, or buttered bread topped with meat and cheese. Along the coasts, many Danes top it with salmon, herring, or even eel!

Danish meatballs, or *frikadeller*, are the national dish. Cooks mix beef, pork, or veal with milk, eggs, and breadcrumbs. Then they flatten the meatballs and cook them. They are often served with potatoes and vegetables.

frikadeller

smørrebrød

National holidays mark important events in Danish history. On June 5, Danes remember the day their country signed its **constitution**. This holiday is called Constitution Day. New Year's Day is also celebrated across the country. Danes watch fireworks and listen to the Queen of Denmark make a speech on New Year's Eve.

Many Danes also observe religious holidays. Most people are Christian and celebrate Christmas and Easter. For Christmas, Danes decorate their cities with lights and Christmas trees. Many also decorate their homes with wreaths and candles.

fun fact

During the holiday season, *aebleskiver* are popular breakfast treats. These balls of baked dough are filled with fruits, sweets, or syrup.

Did you know?

In December, Danish children have special Christmas calendars. Each day on the calendar has a small box to open with a surprise inside. Some boxes are filled with chocolate!

The Vikings

Did you know?
The Vikings were the first Europeans to reach North America. They settled in Newfoundland, which is now part of Canada.

The land within Denmark's borders was once ruled by the Vikings. These fierce warriors and skilled sailors invaded much of the Scandinavian Peninsula from the late 8th century to the 11th century. The Vikings are the ancestors of many Danish people.

Danes have found **artifacts** and shipwrecks from the Viking Age. Many of these are on display in museums. The Viking Ship Museum in Roskilde has five shipwrecks that were recovered from the Roskilde Fjord. Many Danes and tourists go to the museum. The ships and artifacts remind people of Denmark's long history as a strong, enduring country.

fun fact

The Vikings were excellent shipbuilders. They could build wooden ships that were fast and able to withstand the waves and storms of the ocean.

Fast Facts About Denmark

Denmark's Flag

Denmark's flag is called *Dannebrog*, which means "Danish cloth." It is red with a white cross. The red stands for strength and bravery, and the white stands for honesty and peace. First flown in the 14th century, *Dannebrog* is one of the oldest national flags in the world.

Official Name: Kingdom of Denmark

Area: 16,639 square miles (43,094 square kilometers); Denmark is the 133rd largest country in the world.

Capital City:	Copenhagen
Important Cities:	Aarhus, Odense, Aalborg, Frederiksberg
Population:	5,515,575 (July 2010)
Official Language:	Danish
National Holiday:	Constitution Day (June 5)
Religions:	Christian (98%), Other (2%)
Major Industries:	farming, fishing, manufacturing, services
Natural Resources:	fish, farmland, natural gas, oil, limestone, salt
Manufactured Products:	iron, steel, chemicals, food products, clothing, wood products, ships, transportation equipment, electronics, machinery
Farm Products:	barley, wheat, potatoes, sugar beets, dairy products, pork, fish
Unit of Money:	Danish krone; the krone is divided into 100 øre.

Glossary

ancestors—relatives who lived long ago

artifacts—items made long ago by humans; artifacts tell people today about people from the past.

constitution—the basic principles and laws of a nation

diet—the food and drink normally consumed by a person

fjords—long, narrow inlets of ocean water between tall cliffs; the movement of glaciers creates fjords.

Germanic peoples—people from northern Europe who speak the Germanic languages

immigrants—people who leave one country to live in another country

minerals—elements found in nature; copper, silver, and limestone are examples of minerals.

natural resources—materials in the earth that are taken out and used to make products or fuel

Nordic peoples—people from the Nordic area of Europe; this area includes Denmark and the Scandinavian Peninsula.

peninsula—a section of land that extends out from a larger piece of land and is almost completely surrounded by water

service jobs—jobs that perform tasks for people or businesses

shipping lanes—common paths ships travel when they carry people and goods across the sea

straits—narrow waterways that connect larger bodies of water; the Danish Straits connect the Baltic Sea to the North Sea.

territories—areas of land that belong to a country; Greenland and the Faroe Islands are territories of Denmark.

tourists—people who are visiting a country

To Learn More

AT THE LIBRARY

Hansen, Ole Steen. *Denmark*. Austin, Tex.: Raintree Steck-Vaughn, 1998.

Schomp, Virginia. *The Vikings*. New York, N.Y.: Children's Press, 2005.

Stein, R. Conrad. *Denmark*. New York, N.Y.: Children's Press, 2003.

ON THE WEB

Learning more about Denmark is as easy as 1, 2, 3.

1. Go to www.factsurfer.com.

2. Enter "Denmark" into the search box.

3. Click the "Surf" button and you will see a list of related Web sites.

With factsurfer.com, finding more information is just a click away.

Index

The images in this book are reproduced through the courtesy of: Henry Wilson, front cover, pp. 8 (small), 11 (top), 14, 19 (left); Maisei Raman, front cover (flag), p. 28; Jon Eppard, pp. 4-5, 9; Winfried Schofer / Photolibrary, pp. 6-7; Du Boisberranger Jean / Photolibrary, p. 8; Pixtal Images / Photolibrary, pp. 10-11; Marevision / Age Fotostock, p. 11 (middle); Clinton Moffat, p. 11 (bottom); Global Warming Images / Alamy, p. 13; Westend 61 / Photolibrary, p. 14 (small); Jean-Marc Charles / Photolibrary, p. 15; Jonatan Fernstrom / Getty Images, p. 16; NielsDK NielsDK / Photolibrary, p. 17; vario images GmbH & Co.KG / Alamy, p. 18; Masterfile, p. 19 (left); Yadid Levy / Photolibrary, p. 19 (right); Herbert Kratky, p. 20; Norbert Eisele-Hein / Photolibrary, p. 21; Martin Turzak, p. 22; Inga Nielsen, p. 23 (top); Corbis / Photolibrary, p. 23 (bottom); Travel Pix / Photolibrary, pp. 24-25; AFP / Getty Images, pp. 26-27; Morten Kjerulff, p. 29 (bill); Freddy Eliasson, p. 29 (coin).